Impressum / Imprint

Text: AI (Claude Opus, Sonnet), Peter Riegler

Cover: AI (Leonardo, Nano Banana), Peter Riegler

Publisher:

RATONGA® academy

Ratonga Digital GmbH

Siebenlinden 63

3931 Schweiggers

Austria

publish@ratonga.academy

Version: 2026-1.3.12

ISBN: 9783819426339

Herstellung und Druck über tolino media GmbH & Co. KG,

Albrechtstr. 14, 80636 München. Printed in Germany.

Fragen zu Produktsicherheit an: gpsr@tolino.media.

Peter Riegler

The Adventures of Veit the Fox

Chapters:

Chapter 1:

The Forest Home

This is the story of a young fox. His name was Veit, and he made his home in a great forest. It was a nice place to live — calm, simple, and full of peace — and that is where our tale will begin.

Every morning, at the very first light of dawn, Veit would awake and sniff the fresh air. He liked to step outside and walk around, happy to start another day. Veit was small but brave, clever but gentle, and the most curious little creature in all the forest.

He had the ability to have a good time no matter what, and he was able to make any friend smile. His best friend and buddy was a cute rabbit, who kept a nest among the roots of a tall maple tree. He was smart, kind, and keen to help.

When spring came in April, the whole area would bloom. A bright sun filled the sunny sky, and a soft breeze carried the scent of flower and blossom across the meadow. Pretty rose bushes grew upon the hill, and thick bamboo lined the garden path.

"Hello!" called Veit to a dove sitting on a limb. "What a fine morning!" "Welcome to a good day," said the dove.

The forest was full of beauty and life. Veit knew about every creature near his home. The eagle and the hawk would soar high in the sky. The hen and the goose loved the shallow creek. A deer rested in the cool shade of an old oak, while a happy frog sang by the pond. The hedgehog loved to find a nut or a ripe pear under a leaf. A mouse would look for seed and fruit, and a tiny lizard sat on a stick in the dirt. Even the wolf, who roamed the wild outdoor hills, was gentle to Veit.

There, by the creek, a clump of green grass grew beside an olive tree. Honey dripped from a bird nest high above. Old timber and lumber lay on the earth, covered in mushroom caps. A squirrel leaped through the wood, and a goose floated across the pond. Each stem and leaf seemed to glow in the warm light. Nature was quiet and at rest.

Veit loved his hollow oak tree, the early breeze of spring, and the sound of the creek. Autumn would bring a different kind of beauty, but for now he was content.

He did not yet know that his peaceful life was about to change.

Chapter 2:
The Crystal Legend

One evening, Veit began to notice something unusual. A faint glow came from beyond the meadow, from a place he did not know. The light had been absent for as long as anyone could remember, but now it was back. Curious, Veit decided to search for its source.

He followed the glow into a hidden cave at the edge of the forest. He had to enter carefully, for the passage was dark. Inside, the cave was ancient, full of stone and shadow. Above him, the ceiling dripped. Below his feet, the ground was covered in old dust. Between two large rocks, Veit could detect a faint shimmer.

There, on the ground, he found a crystal — broken into three piece fragments. He picked up one piece and held it in his paw. It was fragile and seemed to glow with a strange energy. A crack ran through its center, and each piece seemed to resemble a tiny star.

"What is this?" Veit asked. His voice made a soft echo inside the cave.

Then he began to notice a sign on the wall — a symbol carved in ancient script. Each letter was worn and hard to describe. He also found a book nearby, its page yellow with age. A small note fell from between the pages.

He must open it and seek an answer.

The book told a legend from a forgotten era, a story that went back more than a century, perhaps a decade beyond even that. It spoke of a crystal of rare power — a special artefact with the essence of eternal energy. The crystal was the key to a great force that could protect the entire forest. But a terrible monster — a dragon, some would say, or a ghost of pure darkness — had once cast a spell to crack the crystal and make the piece fragments vanish into obscure and hidden places.

The legend went on: only someone with the spirit and soul of a true seeker could find the pieces and uncover their secret. An ancient ritual was needed to unlock the magic and restore the crystal to its original form. The old book gave a hint — seek the wisdom of the wise Elder Owl, who can reveal what is certain and what is merely myth.

Veit read every word on the page. The message was vague in places, and he could barely explain the meaning of the script, but the evidence was clear: the mystery was real. This was not a fantasy or a dwarf tale told to children. He did not need to ask for proof — the glow in his paw was enough.

Before he left, Veit took one last glimpse at a carving on the wall. It showed a great goddess surrounded by light, and at her side stood a giant figure — half creature, half shadow. The symbol told a story older than history itself.

Veit closed the book and stepped outside. He will discover the truth. He will learn every chapter of this mystery. But first, he needed the advice of the Elder Owl, who was known to speak with a quiet whisper, to tell only what mattered, and to mention things that were unique and special.

"I must find those missing pieces," Veit said. "I must remember every hint and follow every sign."

A glimpse of the moon appeared above the trees. The cave fell silent. The spirit of the legend lingered in the air, as if to say: do not forget. The power of the crystal will appear again — but only to someone brave enough to search for it.

And so, a great quest had begun. Before the next dawn, Veit the fox would embark on a journey unlike any the forest had ever seen.

Chapter 3:
Family & Farewell

Veit knew he could not abandon the quest. The crystal needed him. But before he could depart, he had to talk to his family.

He walked back to the old oak tree, where all the foxes lived together — his mother and father, his brother and sister, and even his aunt and uncle, who had come to visit with their nephew and little cousin. It was a full home, noisy and warm.

His mom sat by the fire, holding an infant in a soft cradle. His dad stood close by, watching a toddler play with a small doll and a wooden toy. A baby fox slept in the corner, peaceful and still. The youngest kid — a shy girl with bright eyes — sat next to her twin brother, who was already half asleep.

Veit looked at they — his family — and felt a wave of emotion wash over him. He would miss every one of them: every man and woman, every boy and girl, every child and adult. The love in this room was strong, and leaving it behind made his heart ache.

"I have something to say," Veit began.

His father raised an eyebrow but did not frown. His mother put down the cradle and turned to listen. His sister stopped humming, and his brother looked up.

"I must go on a journey," Veit said. "I want to find the missing pieces of the crystal, and I believe I can do it."

His mother felt a rush of worry. "Are you sure?" she asked, her voice quiet.

"I am afraid," Veit admitted, and he could feel a blush rise on his cheeks. "But I have faith that it will work out."

His father nodded. "We trust you, Veit. You are no longer naive. Since your birth, I have watched you grow, and I know you are ready."

His aunt wiped a tear. "Please be careful," she said. Her husband turned to his wife and whispered, "He will come back. I am sure of it."

"I agree," said his mother, wrapping her arm around her youngest daughter. "We all agree — Veit can do this."

"Soon," Veit promised. "I will come back soon."

His uncle stepped forward. "Do not regret this choice. And do not leave your hope behind. Always carry it with you, like a lantern in the dark."

The room fell silent. The sadness was heavy, but so was the pride. Veit hugged his cousin, kissed his sister on the forehead with a gentle kiss, and held his mother close. He could feel her heart beating fast.

"Tomorrow," he said. "I leave tomorrow."

"Then today we celebrate," said his mom, trying to smile. "We will not be sad. We will not cry. We will hold on to the dream of seeing you again."

But when night came and the house grew quiet, Veit heard his mother cry softly. The grief of a parent who must let a child go is a deep and tender thing. His sibling lay awake too, each one unhappy and upset at the thought of being apart.

Veit stared at the ceiling. He thought about the marriage of courage and fear that lived inside every heart. He thought about the couple — his mom and dad — who had given him everything. He thought about how, at every age, from infant to adult, a person must sometimes choose to walk a difficult path.

He clutched the crystal piece and made a quiet wish: let me keep my family safe. Let this journey not be in vain.

Outside, the wind whispered through the trees. It seemed to say: go. Do not wait. Do not worry. Your family will always be here. They will never abandon you, and you must never abandon them.

Veit closed his eyes. He was ready. Tomorrow, the journey would begin. And no matter how far apart they might be, love and faith and trust would hold them together, now and always, like a wedding vow that time could never break.

At dawn, he would take his first step. But tonight, he held his family close, and that was enough.

An old orphan once told him: "The strongest bond is not the one you can see — it is the one you feel in your heart, even when you are far away."

Veit would never forget those words.

Chapter 4:
The River Journey

At dawn, Veit set off on his journey. He carried a small bag and a bundle of food, and walked ahead with purpose. The crystal piece in his pocket glowed faintly, as if to guide him forward.

He followed the path south, past fields and fences, until he reached a wide magic river. The water was deep and blue, and the current was strong. Veit could see foam and bubble on the surface, and a gentle ripple spreading from side to side. The river seemed to extend as far as the eye could see.

"I cannot swim across this," Veit said. "The current is too rapid."

Then he spotted a small canoe tied to a bridge. Near it floated a wooden boat, rocking on the water. An old duck sat on the bank, watching the river flow.

"May I paddle your canoe?" Veit asked.

"Of course," said the duck. "But you must be eager and pay attention. The river will carry you forward if you follow the main route. Do not divert from the middle section, or you will drift into the swamp."

Veit climbed into the canoe and began to paddle. The water was cold but smooth, and the boat moved swift and true. He passed a canal lined with tall reeds, and a curve in the river that opened into a wide lake. There, the water became calm and still, like liquid glass.

He saw many creatures during his trip. A salmon leaped out of the water. A silver fish darted below. A tuna broke the surface near a cluster of coral. A lobster hid under a rock, and a shrimp rested on a shell covered in foam. A playful dolphin followed the canoe for a minute or more, while an oyster clung to a stone in the shallow water. Normally, all these animals do not live side by side, but in this magical river, it is possible.

On one island, Veit decided to pause and rest. He pulled the canoe onto the beach and sat on the sand. A turtle crawled slowly past, and Veit could spot a flock of bird on the coast in the distance. A fly buzzed around his ear.

He did not expect the journey to take so long. It had already been an hour, and he still had far to travel. The source of the second crystal piece lay somewhere to the south, in a region he had never visited. He looked at his luggage — just the small bag and bundle — and decided to move on.

"I must not delay," he told himself. "I must hurry. Every minute counts, and time does not wait."

He climbed back into the canoe and continued down the river. The route took him past another island and through a narrow section where the water rushed rapid and fast. He had to orient himself by looking at the sun and the shape of the coast on the left. In front of him, a fishing net hung from a pole, and on the other side, driftwood seemed to float toward the bank.

Later, the river began to merge with a larger stream. The current grew stronger, and Veit had to paddle hard to keep his place in the middle. A frequent splash of wave hit the side of the canoe, and the fluid motion of the water made the small boat rock from side to side.

During the trip, Veit would glance behind to see how far he had come. The forest was now far away. He passed through various landscapes — wet marshes, open plains, and rocky coast. He saw a bridge in the distance and knew his next stop was near.

He would arrive by next morning, he hoped. For now, he would let the river carry him, spend the night under the stars, and prepare for what lay ahead.

The water was his road now. And every turn, every curve, every new place along the way brought him closer to the second piece of the crystal.

Veit was not afraid. He was eager to embark on each new venture, to cross each bridge, and to follow the river wherever it chose to glide. He had left his home a few month ago — though it felt like a lifetime — and the journey was far from over.

He would travel until he found what he was looking for. That was the only way forward.

"Survey the land," the Elder Owl had told him. "Situate yourself by the river, and the water will show you the way."

Veit smiled. The river flowed on, and so did he.

Chapter 5:
The Mountain Challenge

The river had carried Veit far to the south, and now the land began to change. The flat meadows gave way to rocky hills, and in the distance rose a mountain so tall that its top vanished into the clouds. The second piece of the crystal was hidden somewhere up there, and Veit would have to climb to find it.

He stood at the base of the mountain and looked up. The height was enormous. The cliff walls were steep, and the ridge above looked narrow and dangerous. A flash of lightning lit the sky, followed by a low rumble of thunder.

"I must not quit," Veit said, gripping his bag tight. "I must try."

He began to climb. The effort was hard from the start. The rocks were rough and damp, and a thick fog rolled in from the valley below. He could barely see the path ahead. Each inch upward was a struggle, and the danger was real. One fall could mean the end.

Veit had packed a small kit with supplies — a blanket, a torch, and a coil of rope. He wore a warm jacket and kept his eyes on every edge and gap in the rock. He was aware that the weather could change in an instant, so he moved with caution. He was also careful to equip himself properly and cover his ears against the cold. The heavy clouds above looked like an alarm signal.

At one point, the path split into two. Veit chose the left trail, which wound through a tunnel carved into the rock. Inside, the air was cold, and water would drip from the ceiling. He could hear a distant echo that made him want to crouch and hold still. A sudden slide of loose stone made him gasp, and he had to grab a ledge to avoid a nasty tumble. The rock beneath him began to drop away, and for a terrible moment, Veit felt the panic of falling.

But he did not fall. He pulled himself up, muscles aching, and squeezed through a narrow crack. He was tired and could feel the burden of exhaust in every limb. But giving up was not an option.

"I must push on," he whispered. "I must pull myself through."

Behind him, the cloud grew darker. A shadow moved across the mountain, and the thunder rumbled again. The weather was turning harsh. Veit wrapped the blanket around his shoulders and lit the torch. The flame cast a warm glow on the wet stone walls.

He found a small cabin near a camp site, high on a ledge. He decided to rest there until the storm passed , because he did not have a tent with him. He crawled inside and tried to sleep, but the wind howled through every gap and the thunder would not stop.

The mountain was testing him. Every spike of rock, every icy slide, every twist in the path seemed designed to scare him. He had to adjust to the altitude and scale each new obstacle with care. He had to be alert at all times, aware of every hazard — a loose chunk of stone, a hidden hole, a steep drop into the fog below.

He kept climbing. One step at a time. The grit in his heart kept him going when his body wanted to quit. He would not abandon the quest. He had made a promise, and he would hold to it. Some sections would require a ladder made of branches to scale a rocky shaft. He was almost at his limit, but he pushed through. A creature unaware of the danger might have turned back — but not Veit.

On the second day, the fog began to lift. Veit reached the upper ridge and stood at the very top of the mountain. The view was breathtaking — a vast landscape spread out in every direction, and the sun broke through the cloud at last.

There, in a small hollow at the peak, behind a wall of ice, Veit saw it: the second piece of the crystal, glowing with a pale blue light. He had to squeeze past a final edge, clutch the icy wall, and inch forward until he could reach it.

He picked it up. It was cold and smooth, and it hummed with power.

"Two down," Veit said, barely able to breathe. "One to go."

He placed it in his bag beside the first piece, and for a moment the two fragments seemed to glow brighter together. The mountain had tried to surround him with danger, to exhaust him, to make him stumble and fall. But Veit had faced every risk and refused to give up.

He looked out from the mountain top and felt a rush of pride. The scout in him had found the way. The next part of his journey lay beyond the mountain range, and he was not going to stop now.

He made his way down, careful to avoid every loose stone and blur of ice. He would need to find an exit from the mountain pass and continue his quest. But for now, he rested, warmed his hands by a small fire, and watched the flame flicker in the brisk evening air.

The mountain had been the hardest challenge yet. But Veit had conquered it — one step, one inch, one moment of grit at a time.

He was ready for whatever came next.

Chapter 6:
The Village Market

After days of walking, Veit arrived at a small village nestled in a green valley. He was tired and hungry, and the smell of fresh food drifting from every window made his stomach rumble. Today he would rest, fill his belly, and visit the famous morning market.

The village market was a lively place. Every aisle was crowded with color and noise. Long wooden table displays held mountains of fruit: bright red apple, golden banana, purple grape, rosy cherry, pale lemon, sunny orange, soft pear, ripe mango, fuzzy kiwi, green avocado, and crunchy walnut and peanut. One vendor had a tall rack of coconut, and another sold bundles of celery, fresh broccoli, cabbage, onion, and garlic.

Veit picked up a basket and began to collect what he needed. He chose corn, bean, potato, tomato, and a large pumpkin. He added pepper, rice, and wheat bread. A chef behind a counter offered a sample of cheese and a slice of bacon. The taste was wonderful.

"How much does this cost?" Veit asked, pointing at a jar of golden honey.

"Not much at all," said the owner of the stall. "A fair price for good quality."

Veit loved to bargain. He would bid low, the vendor would counter, and they would deal somewhere in the middle. It was all part of the trade. At the village market, you could sell or swap almost anything. The buyer and seller would exchange a handshake, and that was enough.

He stopped at a food stall and ordered lunch. The menu was simple: soup with noodle and meat, a plate of salad with oil and salt, a burger with ketchup and sauce, or a steak with spice and cinnamon ginger glaze. For dessert there was cake, pudding with syrup, jelly on toast, candy, and muffin with cream and sugar. Veit could barely choose — every dish looked delicious.

He sat on a wooden stool next to a large table and pulled up a chair. The chef brought out a tray with his order: a bowl of soup, a crisp green salad, a sausage on a plate, and a tall glass of juice. To drink, he had a cold soda. There was also a pizza with melted cheese, and a portion of beef with vegetables. He was really very hungry after the long journey. Veit used a spoon and fork and a sharp knife to eat. He wiped his mouth with a napkin and tasted every flavor. He left a small tip on the table.

"Would you like some butter on your bread?" asked the cook.

"Yes, please," said Veit. "And a cup of warm milk too."

From the cupboard behind the stove, the cook pulled out a jar of homemade jam — sweet and thick with pulp. He began to boil water for tea and mix herbs into a fragrant mixture for another guest. He added a pinch of salt and a drizzle of oil to the steak still sizzling on the oven. The kitchen smelled of spice and roasted egg, of cereal and caramel syrup. "I prefer fresh ingredients," the cook said. "You can obtain them at the grocery down the road — everything is cheap and honest. Come back for dinner if you like; I will offer you something special." He began to stuff herbs into a roast and wrap it in leaves.

"Thank you," Veit said. "The food here is the best I have ever had."

"You are always welcome," said the old chef, wiping his hands on his apron. "Visit again any time."

At the grocery Veit could not afford everything he wanted, but he had just enough coin to purchase the basics. He picked extra portions of rice and corn, a sack of bean, and a small box of dried meat. He made a list of things to bring on his journey and asked the vendor if he could borrow a cart for the day.

"Of course," the vendor said. "Just put everything in and bring it back by sundown."

Veit loaded the cart with his supplies: fabric and cloth, cotton and silk for a new garment and blouse, plus all the food wrapped in foil. He checked the label on each item to make sure it was right, and folded every material with care before tucking it in. He also found a catalog from the local shop and picked out a few spare tools.

He paid the total amount with his last coin, slid his purse back into his pocket, and smiled. The payment was fair.

The village was warm and kind. Veit liked the way the people lived — they would cook and share, arrange flowers on every windowsill, and treat every stranger like a friend. He noticed a small auction happening at the edge of the square, where a buyer raised his hand to bid on a painted dish. Another stall sold raw fiber and cotton thread, and a third offered bottles of wine from the local vineyard.

After lunch, Veit wrapped a snack of roast walnut and crunch cereal in foil and tucked it into his bag. He folded the cloth, sealed the jar of jelly, and checked that everything was packed. He helped the vendor fold up the stalls and collect the last item from the rack.

Later Veit returned the cart and thanked the villagers once more. He sat at the edge of the village, watching the warm light fade over the valley.

He would need every bit of food and strength for what lay ahead. But for now, he was full and grateful. He picked a last tomato from a vine, wiped it on his sleeve, and took a bite.

It was sweet, and it tasted like home.

He walked on, carrying the warmth of the village with him. In his basket, beside the rice and bread and pepper, lay the two crystal piece fragments, wrapped in soft silk. They glowed faintly in the fading light, as if to satisfy some deep and ancient hunger of their own.

"The recipe for this quest," Veit thought, "is equal parts courage, patience, and good food."

He lend a thought to his family back home, select a direction, and set off once more. The next chapter of his adventure was about to begin.

Chapter 7:
The Ocean Voyage

The road led Veit to the west, to a bustling harbor where tall ships rocked in the wind. The smell of salt filled the air, and the sound of crashing wave echoed along the stone docks. Beyond the harbor, the ocean stretched out, vast and immense, its surface glittering under the afternoon sun.

Veit needed to cross the sea. The third and final piece of the crystal lay somewhere on a distant shore, and the only way to reach it was by water. He walked along the dock until he found a sturdy wooden vessel — a merchant ship with tall masts and a huge painted bow.

A pelican sat on a post nearby, watching him with curious eyes.

"Looking for passage?" called a voice from the deck. It was the captain, a grey cat with a patched coat and a confident grin. "We sail at dawn. The voyage takes three days if the wind holds."

"Where do you go?" Veit asked.

"To the southern coast," the captain said. "We deliver cargo and supply to the village there — barrel of grain, bulk goods, load after load. We take on a draft of new crew at every port. We need a sharp pair of eyes. Can you help direct the lookout?"

"I can," Veit said, and he climbed aboard.

The crew was a rough but friendly bunch: a dutch sailor who told tall tales, a young pilot who could read the stars, and a cook who made the best fish stew on the entire ocean. They showed Veit how to board the rigging, tie a proper knot, and keep watch from the crow's nest.

At sunset, the ship left the harbor. The tide pulled them out, and the sail caught the wind. Veit stood at the bow and watched the land shrink behind him. The ocean was beautiful and terrifying at the same time. The water was so deep that Veit could not imagine its depth — the bottom must be miles below. A large shadow moved beneath the surface, and the colors changed with every passing cloud — from pale green to dark blue to silver. It felt less like a simple crossing and more like a proper cruise across the world.

During the night, a surge of rough water hit the ship. The wave grew tall, and spray lashed the deck. The captain barked orders, and the crew scrambled to pull in the sail. Veit held on tight as the vessel rocked and groaned. For a moment, he feared they might plunge into the deep and wreck upon a hidden reef.

But the storm passed, and by morning the sea was calm again. A whale surfaced near the ship, sending a fountain of mist into the air. A flock of seabirds followed in their wake, calling out in loud voices.

Veit felt the call of the ocean in his heart. It was wild and free, a place of immense beauty and danger. He understood now why sailors loved the sea — it was a world unto itself, vast and full of mystery.

On the third day, land appeared on the horizon. The southern coast shimmered in the haze. The captain gave the order to anchor, and the ship glided into a quiet bay.

"This is your stop," the captain said, shaking Veit's paw. "The marine caves along that cliff — that is where you will find what you seek. But be careful. The tide can surge without warning."

Veit thanked the crew, gathered his things, and climbed down to the shore. The ocean voyage was over, but the hardest part of his quest still lay ahead.

The flight of a lone seabird overhead seemed to point the way.

He took a deep breath of salt air and walked on.

Chapter 8:
The Desert Crossing

Beyond the southern coast, the land changed quickly. The green fields turned yellow, then brown, and then to bare sand. Veit had entered the desert — a vast, empty world of heat and silence that stretched in every direction, from east to west, and seemed to have no end.

The sun beat down without mercy. The sand was flat in some places and rose into tall dune hills in others. Dust swirled around his feet, and a harsh wind blew grit into his eyes. The air tasted dry and carried a faint, sour odor — the smell of nothing growing, nothing alive.

Veit felt the fatigue in his bones. He was hungry, and the heat drained his strength with every step. A feeling of despair crept over him. The desert was awful and bleak, a land of misery where even the ground seemed to crumble under his paws. He could feel the sand erode the soles of his feet. Slow erosion was the desert's weapon — it did not attack, it simply wore you down.

Yet Veit refused to give up. He had learned to adapt to harsh conditions. He traveled at dawn and at dusk, and rested during the hottest hours beneath the palm trees that grew near a dry canyon. He found water in a hollow cactus and ate the bitter seeds of a desert plant.

He was not alone. The desert was home to strange and dangerous creatures. A scorpion hid under a slab of stone, its tail raised to sting. A snake lay coil in the shade, watching Veit with cold eyes. A spider had built a silver web between two rocks, and a cloud of mosquito buzzed overhead. A wasp darted past, and in the distance, a coyote howled at the moon. A swarm of locusts darkened the sky for a brief, weird moment.

Veit pressed on through a maze of rocky canyon walls. He passed a crater from some long-ago erupt of a nearby volcano, and climbed a pyramid of stacked stone that marked the border of an unknown zone. The lava fields beyond were black and cracked, like a scar across the earth.

There were times he felt unable to continue. The glare of the sun was blinding. The gloom of night brought freezing cold. The silence was dumb — it swallowed every sound. He would sometimes feel a burst of energy, only to decline again. The feeling of useless wandering grew stronger, and the endless sand seemed to scatter his courage like dust in the wind. Poverty of spirit is the worst kind of hunger, and out here, in the empty waste of the desert, it was easy to lose hope.

But Veit was a pioneer of the heart. He knew that to divide the journey into small steps was the key to survival. One step, then another. He would not let the desert crush him.

He crossed into a region of exotic jungle at the desert's edge — a hidden oasis where a tribe of friendly travelers lived. They shared their food and stories. Veit had just enough strength left to crawl to the shade. The land around the oasis was vacant and still, but the oasis itself hummed with life. One old traveler warned Veit about a trap set in the sand by bandits, and showed him the safe path through.

"Do not smoke the tobacco plants that grow near the volcano," the traveler said. "They will make you idle and slow."

Veit thanked the tribe and continued through the last stretch of desert. The sand began to decrease at last. The flat ground gave way to rolling hills, and the first green grass appeared.

He looked back at the desert — that terrible, beautiful, empty zone of sand and stone — and felt a surge of pride. It had tried to crush his spirit, to fill him with misery and despair. But he had walked through it, step by step, and he was still standing.

The third crystal piece was near. He could feel it glowing faintly in the distance. Somewhere beyond the next hill, the final part of the puzzle waited.

And Veit was ready.

Chapter 9:
The City of Lights

Veit crossed the last hill and saw it — a city glittering in the distance. Towers of glass and steel rose into the sky, and a web of street and alley spread out in every direction. This was the City of Lights, the biggest, busiest place Veit had ever seen.

He entered through the main gate and stepped into a world of noise and motion. A bus rumbled past, followed by a truck and two taxi cabs. A red car honked at a bicycle, and a bike messenger swerved through the traffic. A van idled at a stoplight, and a sleek black vehicle pulled up to a tall hotel. The street was packed, the subway hummed underground, and a distant siren echoed from somewhere in the urban maze.

Veit had never seen so many people in one place. Every corner had a shop or a bar or an office. A flashing screen displayed the latest news, and a radio played music from an open window. The city was busy and loud, a machine that never stopped.

He walked past a row of buildings: a salon with bright lights, a casino with golden doors, a garage full of auto parts, and a lounge with soft couch seats. He passed a park where children played, and a square where a man stood on a box and talked about the economy. A clock on a tower showed the time, and a lamp flickered on the corner of every street. The town was divided into a neat grid of avenues and lanes. A panel of screens showed train schedules, and a glowing tube sign marked the entrance to the subway.

Veit needed to find work. He had spent his last coin at the village market, and the journey ahead still required supplies. He walked into a small firm and spoke with the boss.

"I can do any job," Veit said. "I earn my keep. I don't need a fortune — just a fair fee for fair work."

The boss — a tall cat in a suit — looked him up and down. "We employ all sorts here, and we hire quickly," she said. "We manage a company that builds and repairs machine parts. We promote good workers and pay a bonus at the end of each month. The wage is fair, and the income is steady. Can you check the stock and keep record of every transfer?"

"I can," Veit said.

He was given an account number, a badge, a card to swipe at the door, and a desk at the corner of the office.

His job was to scan every item that came through, input the data into the system, and report any error. He used a laptop with a glowing screen, connected to a network by a long cable. There was a phone on the desk — he could dial any client — a camera above the door, and a small gadget that beeped every time someone used the elevator. The setup was modern: every device had a plug and a slot for a mobile card. Workers could drive to the office or take the bus. The toilet and break room were down the hall.

He learned quickly. Every day brought new tasks: check the budget, file the report, update the record, cancel a rent payment, process a deposit, handle a loan, review an audit, and manage the weekly schedule. He learned about profit and loss, about credit and asset, about fiscal rate and income changes. The business had to increase its output each quarter to stay competitive. He worked with an analyst who explained the numbers, and a clerk who handled the cash. He would open every envelope of mail, organize the tape in the storage room, and modify the shift plan when a service call came in.

The industry of the city amazed Veit. There were electric trains on the rail, a runway at the airport for flight after flight, a hub where every bus and train route connected, and a ramp leading to the highway. A mechanic in the garage fixed a broken engine and checked the gas gauge. The city would install new utility lines every year, upgrade old systems, and pave the roads smooth. Everyone needed a license to drive, and a video display at the intersection told drivers when to stop. The trash was collected each morning before the city woke. A mechanic in the garage fixed a broken engine, and a robot on the factory floor assembled parts with perfect precision. Every pipe and valve and wire in the city served a purpose. The fuel that powered the motor and the furnace came from far away, delivered by truck and tank and diesel train. A radar dish spun on a rooftop, an antenna reached toward the sky, and a stereo blasted music from a passing car.

The digital age had changed everything. People would click and connect and chat online. They used code to build, program to run, and virtual spaces to meet. A new brand could appear overnight, backed by a clever agent and a strong slogan. The media covered every trend, every advance in technology. Even a thing called satoshi — a small unit of digital value — was traded on the network. The token had become a symbol of the new economy.

Veit worked hard and saved his wage. He made friend with his coworkers, shared coffee in the break room, and even smoked a rare cigar on a Friday evening — though he did not much enjoy it and did it only once. He discovered the gossip and the politics of the office, the demand for results, and the pressure to perform. One day there was talk of a lottery win; another day, a heated debate about the excess output of the factory.

But Veit never forgot his purpose. He invested his earning wisely, bought a ticket for the next train south, and packed his bags. He had used his time in the city to acquire new skills and access new tools. He took the stamp from his work visa, the address of a friend, and a new device that could filter signals and monitor the glow of the crystal pieces.

On his last day, Veit passed a junk yard filled with scrap metal and rubber and old plastic. He passed the indoor market and the garbage trucks, the street performers and the tourist with their camera. He passed the post office, the rail station, the glass towers, and the great city square.

He climbed the ramp to the train platform, found his seat, and settled in. A tenant next to him was reading a paper. A mother held a sleeping child. Outside the window, the city lights began to fade, replaced by open sky and rolling fields.

Veit looked down at the crystal pieces in his bag. They pulsed softly, as if to call him forward. The city had given him much — income, knowledge, and connection — but the quest was not yet over.

The train picked up speed. The wheel clicked over the rail. The urban skyline shrank into the distance, and the night wrapped itself around the world like a great dark blanket.

Veit closed his eyes. He had more to invest — not money, but courage and heart. The final piece of the crystal was waiting, and he would not rest until it was found.

He smiled. The city of light was behind him now, and the last adventure lay ahead.

The switch had been made — from city fox to wanderer once more. And that was exactly where he needed to be.

Chapter 10:
The School of Wisdom

The train carried Veit to a quiet town surrounded by rolling hills. At its center stood a grand old building with tall windows and ivy-covered walls — the School of Wisdom, a place where creatures of every kind came to learn.

Veit did not come here to stay. He came because the Elder Owl had told him that to solve the mystery of the crystal, he would need a deeper understanding of the world. And so, he decided to attend the school for a short while and absorb all the knowledge he could.

On his first day, Veit sat at a wooden desk in a large classroom. A pencil and a pen lay beside a blank sheet of paper. A piece of chalk rested on the ledge of the blackboard. The room was full of young student creatures — some eager, some bored, and a few still half asleep.

The teacher, an old tortoise named Professor, began the lecture.

"Today," she said, "we will define the basic rules of logic and reason. I want you to focus and think. Science is not just about facts — it is about method, about learning how to figure things out. Even the most obvious truth requires inquiry, and a genius is simply someone who refuses to stop asking questions."

The course covered many subject areas. The faculty was excellent, and every lecture was carefully planned. In math, Veit learned to add and multiply, to measure an angle, and to derive a formula using a bracket and an oval shape. He solved puzzle after puzzle, working out the solution to each problem step by step. He practiced until he could get the exact answer on the first try, and learned that a single error could change a result entirely. At initial glance, some problems looked simple, but a minor change in a unit or margin could mean the difference between right and wrong.

"Six times seven equals forty-two," he said aloud. "And eight times twelve is ninety-six. If you multiply ten by twenty, you get two hundred. You can even reach a million if you keep going — or all the way down to zero."

"Correct," said the professor. "Math is a language of precision. Every number has a place, every figure has a meaning."

In biology and science, Veit studied the brain and the mind — how creatures think, reason, and learn. He learned about acid and base, about element and compound. He kept a diary and filled its pages with detail, sketching a diagram of every experiment he performed in the lab. He would edit his notes, review them at night, and repeat what he had learned.

The library was his favorite place. Shelves of book lined the walls, and every title held a new idea. He read fiction and essay, novel and poem. A famous poet had once written that wisdom is not what you know, but what you ask. A great author had said that to educate one mind is to light a fire that will never go out. Veit loved every quote. He also learned to write well — to form a clear phrase, choose the right type of word, and sort his thoughts before putting pen to paper. The usage of common term and brief sentence made any essay easily understood.

He also attended a seminar on ethics — the study of right and wrong. The topic was abstract and sometimes hard to clarify, but the discussions were lively. "Is it normal to assume the best in people?" one student asked. "That depends," said the teacher. "Neither blind trust nor constant suspicion is the correct method. You must consider the actual facts and verify them. A typical example might differ from a random sample, so never guess when you can measure."

"To behave with ethics," the professor added, "is to pay attention to every aspect of a situation — not just the obvious parts. Such inquiry builds character, rather than mere knowledge."

Each session ended with a short quiz or test. The professor would indicate a category — perhaps latin roots, or the history of language — and the pupil who answered first would earn a gold star. Even a junior student could win if they were quick. Some pupils liked to cram the night before, but Veit preferred to study a little each day. He would sort every object by size, arrange every cube on the shelf, and check the index at the back of every book. He found nothing boring — every subject held a secret worth uncovering. Veit was not always the fastest, but he was thorough. He would never omit a detail or give a vague answer when a valid one was required.

The school also had a practical side. Veit learned to copy a document and print it, to use scissors to cut a paper segment, and to glue a broken model back together. He worked on a project that combined science and art, building a small device out of wire and wood. "Every skill matters," said the teacher. "Talent is useful, but practice is what makes you a master."

On the final day, Veit took his last exam — a long test that covered every subject and topic he had studied. He read every question carefully, wrote a clear sentence for each answer, and checked his work twice. The text was dense, but Veit knew the material well. He wrote about the process of erosion, the theory of gravity, and the level of oxygen in the atmosphere. He explained the average length of a river and the width of a mountain range. He described the primary colors, the ordinary rules of grammar, and the similar patterns found in every version of the same old story.

He used every verb he knew. He drew a diagram with care. He felt sure of every answer.

The result came quickly. He had passed with honors.

"You have a sharp brain, young fox," said Professor. "Never stop asking the question that matters most: why? The interest you show today will shape the mind you carry tomorrow. Your degree is not just a document — it is a promise to keep learning."

Veit nodded. He slipped the crystal pieces from his bag and showed them to the professor. The old tortoise studied them through a magnifying lens, turning each one in her wrinkled hands.

"Fascinating," the professor murmured. "These fragments fit a model I once read about in a manual from the old era. The crystal is not just a symbol of power — it is a key to balance. When the three pieces combine, they create a total harmony of energy and matter."

"How do I combine them?" Veit asked.

"That, my dear student, is the final lesson — one you must learn not from a book, but from experience. The solution is inside you. You must identify it for yourself. No one can teach you this — you must drill down into your own heart and think."

Veit thanked the professor and gathered his things — the pencil and pen, the diary, and his well-worn bag. He had come to the school with question marks and left with quiet confidence. He would carry the lesson of this place with him forever.

It was easy to enroll in a school, he thought. The tuition was small and the schedule was regular. But to truly learn

— to let knowledge change you at the minimum — that required something no school could provide: a curious mind and a willing heart.

He walked out into the sunlight. Somewhere ahead, the final chapter of his quest awaited. And he was ready.

"Short or long, easy or hard," Veit said, "the journey is the real teacher."

He set off, carrying the weight of wisdom and the lightness of hope, and never looked back.

Chapter 11:
The Music Festival

Veit arrived at the coastal village on a warm Saturday afternoon, just in time for the annual festival. Bright banner flags hung from every lamppost, and the sound of music filled the air. It was a celebration of art, culture, and fun — a full weekend of dance, song, and laughter.

The main stage stood at the center of a great open arena. A crowd of creatures had gathered, dressed in their finest clothes. Some wore a colorful dress or a flowing skirt, others a casual pair of jeans and a silly hat. One clown near the entrance wore a bright pink ribbon and juggled oranges, making the children giggle and chuckle with delight.

"Welcome to the Festival of Lights!" called the host, a cheerful parrot with a booming voice. "Tonight we celebrate music, drama, and the talent of our finest artist performers. Please clap your hands, enjoy the show, and have a merry time!"

The first act was a jazz band. A tall heron played the piano, a badger strummed a guitar, and a squirrel blew a gleaming trumpet. The melody rose and fell, filling the venue with rich, vibrant sound. The rhythm was smooth and the tone was warm. The volume swelled during the chorus, and the crowd began to sway. A young actress with a powerful vocal range stepped forward and began to sing a ballad — her voice was amazing, vivid, and full of emotion.

"Awesome!" shouted a fan from the front row.

The next episode was a comedy show. A famous actor and a comic walked onto the stage together. They told one joke after another — some funny, some absurd, some so silly that even the critic in the back row had to laugh. The actor would imitate the voices of well-known characters, and the comic would shrug and pull a face. The humor was light and easy, and the crowd was thoroughly amused.

During a short break, Veit explored the festival grounds. There was a gallery full of artwork — paintings in every color, from deep yellow to bright red. A potter shaped wet clay on a spinning wheel, and nearby a young artist used a brush and canvas to draw a scene of rolling hills. Another stall offered handmade craft and pottery. Veit admired the pattern on a painted vase and the design of a woven frame.

"You have real talent," Veit told the potter.

"Art is my hobby and my life," the potter replied with a wink. "I like to express what I feel through clay and color. Every genre is worth exploring."

Veit also visited a small museum nearby. Inside, a special exhibit showed the history of music and fashion through the ages. Old drum sets, faded concert photo prints, and handwritten lyrics hung on the walls. A film clip played on a screen, showing a black-and-white movie from a bygone era. An album cover framed in glass caught Veit's eye — the image was vivid and striking, a true icon of culture.

He stopped at a display of mixed art — sculpture, paint, and light combined in a single feature that seemed to evoke wonder in everyone who looked at it. A small card beneath it read: "This piece is a visual render of sound — an attempt to attract the eye the way music attracts the ear."

"That is the most popular thing in the museum," whispered a guide.

As evening fell, the festival came alive once more. A parade wound through the street, full of dancers, musicians, and performers in colorful mask and costume. An opera singer filled the night with a haunting melody. Veit watched from the fringe of the crowd, tapping his foot to the rhythm.

Then the final act began. A lone violinist walked onto the stage carrying a beautiful violin. She played with such grace and power that the entire crowd fell silent. Every note was a scene — a picture painted in sound. The music told a story of romance and loss, of hope and return. It was a series of emotion captured in melody, and it was the most beautiful thing Veit had ever heard.

When it ended, the crowd erupted. They stood and cheered and threw flowers onto the stage. The fame of the violinist was well earned. Veit felt tears in his eyes. The music had touched something deep inside him — something he could not name but would never forget.

Later, at a quiet corner of the venue, Veit sat with a warm drink and listened to a group of creatures sing old folk songs in an acoustic style. A fox with a small tattoo on his paw played a favorite tune, and the crowd began to clap along. Someone called out: "Come join the party!" Another voice, loud and cheerful, tried to invite everyone nearby. The musicians played something crazy and fast, and the dancers spun in circles. Veit noticed they all wear flowers in their fur. He was in no hurry.

This was his holiday, his moment of leisure and relax. He wore a new hat he had bought at the market, and for the first time in weeks, he felt truly at peace.

He pulled out the crystal pieces and held them up to the lantern light. They sparkled with color — deep blue, pale gold, soft pink — as if the music itself had filled them with new life.

"Even a crystal," Veit thought, "can be moved by a beautiful song."

He tucked them safely away, gave a small clap of appreciation to the last performers, and walked back through the glowing festival grounds. The night was warm, the crowd was happy, and the world felt full of wonder.

Tomorrow the quest would resume. But tonight, he would dance, laugh, and enjoy the simple magic of art and music.

He could hear the drum beat fading in the distance. He sketch a small drawing of the stage in his diary, smiled, and closed his eyes.

What an amazing night. What a vivid, vibrant, awesome festival.

Veit would never decorate a room or paint a picture without thinking of this place. The theme of the festival — that beauty lives in every sound, every image, every color — would stay with him forever.

Chapter 12:
The Hospital

The next morning, Veit woke feeling strange. His head ached, his body felt heavy, and a dull fever burned behind his eyes. He tried to stand, but a wave of dizzy nausea knocked him back down. His pulse was fast, his nose was blocked, and every muscle in his leg and arm throbbed with pain.

"I am ill," Veit whispered, touching his face. His skin was hot to the touch. Even lifting a finger was an effort.

A kind hedgehog found him lying by the road and helped him to the nearest hospital — a clean white building with wide doors and quiet halls. A nurse in a blue uniform met them at the entrance and checked his pulse and temperature.

"You have a high fever and signs of illness," she said. "We need to see a doctor right away."

The doctor, a calm old badger with round spectacles, examined Veit carefully. He looked at Veit's eye and eyebrow, his tongue and tooth, his neck and shoulder, his elbow and wrist, his knee and ankle, his hip and toe, and even pressed gently on his rib and stomach. He checked Veit's skull with a small light and listened to his breathing.

"You have an injury to your left foot — it is infected," the doctor said. "Your immune system is fighting hard, but you also show a symptom of a virus. There is slight swelling near the kidney area, and your blood pressure is low. I also notice a chronic pain in your bone and nerve endings — likely from exhaust and poor diet."

Veit lay on a bed in the clinic while the nurse cleaned and bandaged his foot. She gave him a dose of medicine — a small pill to reduce the fever and fight the infection. She used a razor to trim the fur around the wound, and a syringe to inject a clear fluid.

"Try to inhale slowly and deeply," she said. "Your lung needs oxygen. This organ is vital for recovery."

Veit did as he was told. He felt the flush of warmth return to his face and hand. His pulse began to steady. The pain in his leg and arm eased a little. The tissue around the wound began to heal.

"Health is not something to take for granted," said the doctor, sitting beside Veit's bed. "Your body is strong, but you must take care of it. Watch your diet — eat less fat and more fresh food. Rest when you are tired, and do not ignore a symptom — even a slight one. Medicine can expire, so always check the date. A small habit of care each day can prevent disease and disorder in the future."

Veit nodded. He had pushed himself too hard. He had ignored the pain in his foot, the ache in his hair-thin nerve endings, and the faint warning signals his body had been sending. He had been blind to his own needs.

He stayed in the hospital for three days. The nurse and doctor were kind and patient with him. A donor had provided fresh blood for the clinic, and the medicine worked quickly. Veit's fever broke on the second night, and by the third morning he could stand, walk, and even smile again.

"You are a good patient," said the nurse. "Most foxes are not so calm."

"I have learned to be patient in more ways than one," Veit said.

He also met a young rabbit in the clinic who suffered from asthma and had trouble breathing. Another creature had an anxiety disorder and could not sleep. A third was an addict struggling to give up alcohol. Veit listened to their stories and realized that illness comes in many forms — some you can see, and some you cannot.

"Every creature carries a hurt somewhere," the doctor told him. "Some in the body, some in the mind. The important thing is to seek help and never feel ashamed."

On his last day, the doctor handed Veit a small card. "If you feel sick again, or if the impulse to push too hard returns, stop and rest. You do not need to be slim or fast or perfect — you just need to be well."

Veit thanked him. He looked down at his bandaged foot, flexed his thumb and finger, and took a deep breath.

He was healed. Not just in body, but in spirit.

The hospital had reminded him of something important: the quest was nothing without health, and health was nothing without care.

He stepped outside into the sunlight, feeling the warmth on his skin and the fresh air in his lung. The crystal pieces hummed softly in his bag, as if glad to have him back.

The journey continued. But now Veit walked with more sense — more aware of his body, more grateful for every step, and more determined than ever to see the quest through to the end.

His dentist back home had always told him: "Take care of your tooth, and your tooth will take care of you." Veit smiled at the memory. Perhaps the same was true of everything — body, mind, and soul.

He walked on, one careful step at a time.

Chapter 13:
The Night Sky

That evening, Veit climbed a small hill and lay down on the soft grass. The sun had set, and the sky was turning from deep blue to black. One by one, the stars appeared — tiny points of light scattered across the void like diamonds on dark velvet.

It was a clear night, and the moon hung full and bright above the horizon, casting a pale lunar glow over the land. Veit could see the faint band of the Milky Way stretching across the sky — a galaxy of a million stars, each one a distant sphere of fire.

He pulled out a small lens — a gift from the professor at the School of Wisdom — and held it up to his eye. Through it, the stars became sharper and brighter. He could observe the rings of a far-off planet, the slow orbit of a moon around it, and the faint shimmer of cosmic dust drifting through space.

"How vast the universe is," Veit whispered. "And how small I am."

He thought about the atom — the tiniest building block of all matter. Every element in his body, every bit of carbon in his bones, had once been forged inside a star. He was, in a way, made of starlight. The core of every star burned with the same energy that flowed through the crystal pieces in his bag.

A shooting star streaked across the sky — a brief flash that made Veit gasp with wonder. He tried to predict where the next one would appear, but the sky kept its secrets. The stars seemed to rotate slowly overhead as the earth turned beneath him, following a cycle as old as time itself.

He noticed a cluster of bright stars forming a familiar pattern — a circle of light near the northern axis of the sky. Nearby, a faint cloud of vapor glowed with an eerie green hue — the last trace of ozone catching the lunar light. It seemed to hover in the darkness, fade, and then reappear.

Veit thought about the creatures who had walked this earth long before him — the great dinosaur that once roamed the plains, now nothing but fossil and bone buried deep underground. He thought about ecology — the delicate layer of life that wrapped around the globe like a thin shell. He thought about nuclear energy and solar power, about the forces that held the universe together and the gravity that kept his feet on the ground.

He wondered if somewhere out there, beyond the farthest planet, in the outer reaches of the universe, an alien creature was looking up at the same sky and feeling the same wonder. Perhaps one day a rocket would carry a traveler into the great vacuum of space, past every star and moon, to gaze upon new worlds. At the quantum level, everything was connected — every atom, every mass of matter, held together by forces as invisible as a magnet. And the universe would recycle its own energy, turning old stars into new ones, over and over, forever.

"The universe does not care if we exist," Veit said softly. "But we care. And that is what makes us special."

The night deepened. A soft wind carried the scent of grass and earth. Veit wrapped his blanket around himself and watched the moon climb higher. The spatial arrangement of the stars — the way they filled the void with light — was the most beautiful matrix he had ever seen. Every star was part of a pattern, a cycle of birth and death that repeated across the cosmos.

He thought about the hybrid nature of his quest — part adventure, part discovery, part something he could not name. The crystal was not just a magic object. It was a piece of the universe itself, a fragment of the energy that flowed through everything.

Veit closed his eyes. Tonight, under the black sky, he felt connected to something larger than himself. The alpha star — the brightest in the sky — seemed to shine just for him, a beacon in the darkness.

He would sleep now, and dream of stars.

By midnight, the world was still. The moon cast long shadow across the hill. Somewhere in the distance, an owl called.

Veit reflect on his journey — every step, every challenge, every friend he had made along the way. The crystal pieces pulsed softly in his bag, responding to the lunar light.

Tomorrow, he would walk on. But tonight, the night sky was enough.

The sight was magnificent. The universe stretched on forever, and Veit was a small but brave part of it.

He smiled, and the stars smiled back.

Chapter 14:
The Farm & Animals

The road led Veit through green fields and rolling hills to a large farm surrounded by a wooden fence. A rusty belt held the gate shut, and a broom leaned against the porch. The air smelled of hay and rain and warm animal fur.

This was the home of Old Gruff, a robust goat who had worked the land for decades. He welcomed Veit with a firm handshake and a bowl of fresh soup.

"Rest here," said Gruff. "You look like you could use a good, healthy meal and a dry shed to sleep in."

Veit thanked him and looked around. The farm was alive with creatures. A dog barked at the gate. A cat dozed on a windowsill. A horse stood in the stable, chewing hay beside a stubborn mule and a small brown pony. A donkey brayed from the yard, and a flock of chicken scratched in the dirt. A fat pig wallowed in mud, and a row of cattle grazed in the field beyond the fence.

Veit helped with the daily task of farm life. He would feed the animal every morning, carrying buckets of grain from the barn. He learned to milk a cow, clean the stable, and scrub a muddy shoe on the porch step. He fixed a clog in the water pipe, mended a patch on the roof, and used a hammer to straighten a fence post. It was hard labor, but honest and satisfying.

"Farm life is not lazy," said Gruff. "It takes effort and patience. You must raise the crop, harvest the grain, and produce enough to last the winter. You must wash the wool, trim the hedge, and keep the lawn neat. The season decides everything — in summer, you grow; in autumn, you harvest; in october and august, the days are long and full."

Veit discovered that the farm was also a kind of sanctuary for animal of all kinds. In the orchard beyond the barn, a parrot sat in a tree, mimic the sound of every creature nearby. A raccoon peeked out from behind a bush. A hamster ran in circles on a wheel. A kitten chased a butterfly, and a puppy rolled in the grass. A crane stood tall by the pond, watching for fish, and a raven perched on the fence, dark and silent.

Gruff also cared for wilder creatures. A leopard with a wounded paw rested in a shaded pen. A young tiger paced back and forth, waiting to be released. A lion lay calmly in the sun, and a gorilla sat in the shade, eating fruit. A giraffe stretched its long neck to reach the highest branch. A panda munched on bamboo, and a buffalo stood alone in the far field. A kangaroo hopped past, and an ostrich raced along the fence line. A jaguar watched from the shadows, and a panther moved like a shadow through the trees. Even a tortoise plodded slowly across the yard, its shell worn smooth with age. A monkey swung from a rope, and a zebra stood quietly beside the pond. Nearby, a weasel darted under a log, and a cricket chirped in the tall grass. A swarm of insect buzzed around a bulb of light on the porch, and a mammal of some kind — perhaps a mule — grunt softly in its sleep.

Every creature had a story. Every wing and claw and tail and horn told of a life lived in the wild. Gruff's farm was a place where the wounded could heal and the lost could find shelter.

"We do not own these creatures," Gruff said. "We care for them. And often, they care for us in return."

Veit spent three peaceful days at the farm. He learned to ride the horse, chase a runaway chicken, and fetch water from the well. He helped pluck feathers from a turkey, churn butter, and scrub the pots with soap after dinner.

He would snap green bean for soup and hunt for mushrooms in the rural woods beyond the orchard. He used every tool in the barn — a sharp blade for cutting rope, a hammer for nails. Smoke rose from the chimney as dinner cooked inside. One afternoon, Veit packed a picnic and sat under a tree while a buzz of bees hummed around a flower bed.

A female deer — a gentle doe — would sometimes spawn near the field at dawn, her fawn close behind. An elephant from a nearby ranch had been rescued from a traveling zoo, and now lived peacefully in a wide pen — no longer in a cage but free to roam. Veit liked to sit on the porch, pet the dog, and watch the creatures go about their day beneath a broad umbrella of shade: the slow crawl of the tortoise, the slender leap of the leopard, the patient waddle of the pig. A pile of golden wheat dried in the sun.

He even did the laundry, hanging cloth on a line to dry in the warm summer breeze. He wore an old brown shirt and used a patched apron. Life here was usual and simple, the kind of life he had known back home.

On his last evening, Veit sat with Gruff on the porch. A pigeon cooed on the roof, and a swallow swooped low over the field. The mesh of the screen door kept the bugs out while the warm air drifted in.

"You carry something important," Gruff said, looking at the crystal pieces. "I can see it in your eyes. Whatever it is, remember: the land will always welcome you back. The farm will always be here."

Veit thanked the old goat. He patted the dog, scratched the cat behind the ear, and gave the horse one last apple. He placed his saddle bag over his shoulder, stepped over the wagon rut in the mud, and walked down the road.

The animal watched him go. The dog barked once. The parrot called out a farewell. And the crane lifted from the pond, spreading its great wing against the sky.

The farm was behind him now. But its lessons — of patience, labor, and care — would travel with him to the end.

A resource of strength he did not know he had now lived in his heart.

Chapter 15:
Sports Day

Veit's path led him through a wide valley to a stadium packed with cheering creatures. Colorful flags snapped in the wind, and the roar of the crowd carried for miles. It was Sports Day — the biggest annual competition in the region — and every athlete from every corner of the land had come to compete.

"Welcome!" called a cheerful beaver at the gate. "Would you like to join the game? We need one more member for the relay team."

Veit had never been a great athlete, but he was no amateur either. He was fit, fast, and eager to test himself. He decided to engage.

"I will give it my best," he said.

The opening event was a race — a quick sprint around the track. Veit crouched at the starting line, heart pounding. The whistle blew, and he began to run. His legs pumped, his arms swung, and the wind rushed past his ears. He felt the pure motion of his body, every muscle working in harmony. He dashed past a rabbit, leaped over a hurdle, and crossed the finish line in second place.

"Not bad for a fox!" shouted his coach, a tough old bear. "You have speed and balance. With a little practice, you could be a champion."

The stadium buzzed with action. In one corner, a pair of badgers played tennis, swinging rackets with dynamic force. In another, a team of otters splashed through a pool in a swim race. A kangaroo took a running jump and cleared the bar with room to spare. A deer gave a daring flip off the high platform and landed perfectly.

On the main field, the soccer match was in full swing. One team wore blue, the other red. A fox — Veit's distant cousin — delivered a powerful kick that sent the ball sailing into the goal. The crowd erupted. "Goal!" they screamed. "What a strike!"

The referee blew the whistle for halftime. "Strategy is everything," the coach told his team. "You must aim for the target, time your tackle, and use your position on the field. A quick shuffle can beat a slow defender. A good toss or throw at the right moment can change the game."

After soccer, the events continued at a furious pace. A group of young foxes performed a gymnastics routine in the main arena — some moves were graceful, others a bit awkward, but the crowd loved it. One performer did a trick on the parallel bars that earned a super score from the judges. Another took a stumble and landed on the bench, but got up laughing. There was a hockey match on the ice rink — fast, rough, and thrilling. A boxing round where two bears traded punch after punch. A wrestle contest where a wolf pinned a bear in under a minute. A spin class in the gym that left everyone breathless. And an aerobic exercise session that tested everyone's fitness and endurance. A rally of supporters chanted in the stands, urging their favorites to play harder and win. To achieve victory, every athlete had to tilt the odds in their favor.

Veit tried his hand at everything. He played a round of dice and got lucky. He hit a pitch with a wooden bat, scored a double, and earned a cheer from the crowd. He learned to catch and throw a ball, to swing a racket, to bounce off the ropes, and to slam a volleyball with force. A tag game in the field had everyone laughing and shouting.

The final event was the relay. Veit was the last runner — the anchor. He stood at the track, watching his teammates dash one by one. The rival team was fast, and the match was close. A rival runner surged ahead, and for a moment it looked hopeless.

Then the baton reached Veit's hand. He sprint with everything he had, legs pumping, eyes fixed on the finish line. He kick the dust behind him and leaned forward. The crowd held its breath. The two runners were neck and neck — and then, at the very last second, Veit crossed the line.

"Victory!" screamed the announcer. "What a finish!"

Veit collapsed on the track, gasping for air. His team rushed to him, lifting him onto their shoulders. A gold medal was placed around his neck, and a gleaming trophy was handed to the team captain. A sponsor from the nearby town presented the prize — a beautiful crystal cup that sparkled in the sunlight.

"You are a true champion," said the coach, shaking Veit's paw. "You gave maximum effort and never gave up. That is what makes a winner."

Veit stood on the podium, looking out at the stadium. The crowd cheered, and the sun shone warm on his fur. He felt a boost of pride — not just for the medal, but for every step of the journey that had brought him here.

He had learned that sport was not just about physical strength. It was about balance, strategy, and the courage to engage when the odds were against you. It was about the loop of effort and reward, the excite of the match, and the joy of being part of a team.

In the gym afterward, Veit put on his helmet and tried a kite surfing class — a wild, dynamic ride that sent him soaring over the pool. He laughed, shouted, and felt truly alive.

He left the stadium with the medal around his neck and the crystal pieces safe in his bag. The sport club members waved goodbye, and a rookie runner jogged alongside him for a while, asking for tips.

"Just run," Veit said with a smile. "And never quit."

The road stretched on, and Veit walked with a new spring in his step. The olympic dream of greatness lived in every creature — not just the fastest or the strongest, but in anyone willing to try.

Every action counts. Every aim matters. Every game is worth playing.

Chapter 16:

The Castle & Kingdom

The journey continued the next day. The road climbed steeply, and at its peak stood the most magnificent sight Veit had ever seen: a castle of white marble and grey stone, its tall tower rising high above a walled city. Banners of gold and silver flew from every turret, and a great iron gate guarded the entry. Two soldiers in gleaming armor and polished brass helmets stood at attention, each holding a sword and a shield.

"State your name and your duty," one of the guard called.

"My name is Veit," he said. "I carry pieces of the ancient crystal and seek an audience with your leader."

The guard exchanged a glance. "You may enter," the senior one said, pressing a heavy badge to the lock. The gate swung open with a groan of iron.

Veit stepped inside. The castle was enormous. The floor was laid with patterned carpet and smooth brick. Great column of stone held up a high ceiling painted with scenes of battles and feasts. A curtain of deep red velvet hung from every arch, and a mirror in a gold frame reflected the light of a hundred candles. An antique chest filled with jewel and diamond sat beneath a window of colored glass. A cushion of ivory silk rested on a carved chair, and a thick rug covered the marble floor. The room smelled of cedar and old brass.

The kingdom was ruled by a wise and just chief Queen, a noble fox of royal blood. She sat upon a throne of bronze and steel, wearing a gown of elegant blue and a crown of silver. Her presence radiated dignity and glory.

"Welcome, young traveler," the Queen said. "I have heard of your quest. The crystal is a matter of great importance to this nation."

Veit bowed. "Your Majesty, I carry two of the three pieces. I believe the third is hidden somewhere within your domain."

The Queen nodded. "You are correct. The final piece lies in the vault beneath this castle, guarded by law and custom for over a thousand years. But I cannot simply grant you access. There are rules — legal and civil — that I must obey."

She explained the situation. The crystal was considered public property of the kingdom, protected by a mandate from the congress of elders. To release it would require a formal vote, an order from the federal council, and the approval of the people. It was a complex affair of state, governed by strict rule and tradition. The capital city operated under supreme law, and no one could dismiss a ruling or impose a new one without due process. The council had the power to enact and execute any decision, and a system of security and patrol kept the kingdom safe. Every nominee for the council was chosen through a social contract, and no private interest could control the outcome.

"The law must be followed," said the Queen's deputy, a stern badger in a dark uniform. "We cannot simply allow one person to claim the crystal. The issue must be brought before the forum. We are oblige to reform when needed, but never to act in haste."

Veit understood. He was asked to present his case in a grand debate before the congress. He stood at the center of a great hall, surrounded by citizen from every walk of life — noble lords and peasant farmers, rich merchants and humble maid servants, senior advisors and young bachelor aides. A census had been taken; every person was accounted for.

He spoke with honesty and passion. He told them about the legend, the quest, and the danger that would come if the crystal remained broken. He argued that the kingdom would benefit, that the crystal's power was meant for the people, not for any one leader or elite group.

The congress listened. A general in brass buttons stood to endorse Veit's plea. A notable scholar confirm the crystal's history. Others voiced their opinion — some in favor, some neutral, some opposed. The debate was long, but fair.

At last, the Queen called for a vote. Every citizen raised a hand. The result was clear: they would approve the release, but with one condition. Veit must conduct himself with honor, submit to the laws of the kingdom, and uphold the values of the nation. He must inform the council of every step, and enforce the ancient custom of returning the crystal once it had served its purpose.

"I permit you to take it," the Queen said. "But remember: liberty comes with duty, and wealth is nothing without pride and dignity."

She gave the order, and the guard escorted Veit down a spiraling stairs to the deep vault. The walls were lined with copper and iron, and a thick door of solid steel stood at the end. A lock of ancient design held it shut. The chief of the guard turned the key, and the door swung open.

Inside, on a pedestal of polished marble, the third crystal piece glowed with a brilliant light. Veit reached out and took it. It was warm in his paw, and the moment it touched the other two pieces, a pulse of energy rippled through the room.

"It is done," Veit whispered.

He climbed back up the stairs and stepped onto the balcony of the castle. Below him, the people of the kingdom had gathered. They filled the street and the square, their faces turned upward. The flag of the nation waved proudly above the roof of the great mansion — a palace of luxury and vintage charm — across the road. A fancy ring of flowers decorated the balcony. An old gospel hymn drifted from a nearby chapel. The sunlight caught the gold of the turrets and the bronze of the wall carvings. A lady in a fine dress waved from a window.

Veit held up the three crystal pieces. The crowd gasped. The Queen stood beside him, her gown shimmering in the light.

"This kingdom has done a noble thing today," the Queen announce. "We have chosen to trust, to share, and to govern with grace. Let this be a major moment in our history. I salute this brave young fox."

The people cheered. The guard stood at attention and salute. The staff of the castle — from the highest deputy to the lowliest maid — gathered in the courtyard. A soldier beat a drum, and the metal gate was thrown open to allow the public in.

Veit looked out over the kingdom — the rolling estate of farmland, the distant tower of the city, the great wall that protected it all — and felt a wave of gratitude. Generations of human and creature alike had worked to build this country, to cement its foundations and inherit its traditions. This place, with its marble halls and velvet curtain, its ancient law and living custom, had given him the final piece.

He was ready. The crystal was whole. And the journey home could begin.

He tucked the three pieces into his bag, bowed to the Queen, and walked down the stairs, through the gate, and out into the fading light.

The castle grew smaller behind him. But its glory — and the dignity of its people — would stay with him forever.

He had one thing left to do.

A knock on the door of destiny. And the courage to open it.

He took a deep breath, and walked on.

Chapter 17:
The Arctic Expedition

The journey home took Veit north, far beyond the green valleys and into a land of ice and silence. It was december, and the world had turned white. Winter had arrived, and with it came the bitter cold of the arctic.

Snow fell in thick curtains from a grey sky. The ground was frozen solid, and frost covered every branch and stone. A layer of slush crunched beneath Veit's paws, and powder fine as dust blew across the open plains. The wind cut through his fur like a blade, and he was grateful for his thick jacket, his warm glove, and the hood pulled tight over his ears. He wore a pair of dry sock inside his boots and wrapped a scarf around his face.

The land was vast, empty, and silent. Not a bird sang. Not a creature stirred. Veit felt alone and lonely for the first time on his journey. A shiver ran through his body. The polar landscape stretched endlessly — nothing but ice and snow and sky. He passed a frozen lake, its surface rigid and still, reflecting the pale light like a mirror. A wooden pole marked the edge of a trail, half-buried in drifts.

He wanted to stay and rest, but he knew he must keep moving. To remain still in the arctic was to freeze. He had to push through, one step at a time, even when his legs ached and his body screamed to stop.

On the second day, the snow eased and the clouds parted. A pale sun like in february appeared, low on the horizon, casting long blue shadows over the ice. Veit found a frozen pond and dared to skate across it, sliding on the smooth surface with a mix of fear and joy. On the far side, a slope of packed snow led down a gentle hill, and he took the chance to ski down it on two flat pieces of bark, laughing as the cold air rushed past.

The cold could not isolate his spirit. Even here, in the most frozen corner of the world, Veit felt the crystal pieces humming in his bag — three fragments, now whole in purpose, waiting to be joined. Their warmth pushed back against the frost, a tiny fire against the endless white.

On the third day, the ice began to melt. A trickle of water appeared between the rocks. The air softened. The snow thinned. Green patches of grass peeked through the white.

Veit was leaving the arctic behind. Ahead, the familiar hills of home rose gently against the sky.

He pulled down his hood, tucked his glove into his pocket, and smiled.

He was almost home.

Chapter 18:
The Storm & Conflict

Veit was only a day's walk from home when the sky turned dark. A tornado of black cloud swirled on the horizon, and the wind howled with a terrible fury. Lightning split the sky, and a blast of thunder shook the ground. The storm was drastic — the worst Veit had ever seen.

But the storm was not the only danger.

From behind a ridge of broken rock, a figure emerged — tall, cloaked, and armed with a long sword. It was the Shadow, the enemy Veit had been warned about since the beginning of his quest. The creature's eyes burned with anger, and its voice was cold and cruel.

"Give me the crystal," the Shadow demanded. "Or face your demise."

Veit stood his ground. "I will not. The crystal belongs to everyone."

The Shadow snarled. "Then I will take it by force."

What followed was a battle unlike anything Veit had experienced. The Shadow attacked with a fury born of jealous rage, swinging its sword and firing an arrow from a dark bow. It carried a gun — no, a pistol — and even a rifle slung over its back, along with a cannon mounted on a cart. Bullet flew through the air. The blast of the cannon sent debris flying in every direction.

Veit had no weapon. He had only his wits, his courage, and the crystal's faint glow. He dove behind a boulder to escape the first assault. The impact of the blast knocked him sideways. The crash of stone around him was deafening.

"You cannot flee forever!" the Shadow shouted. "Deny it all you want — the crystal's power is mine to claim!"

Veit refused to give in. He would defy the Shadow, resist every attack, and defend the crystal with his life. The Shadow tried to bind him with chains, to inflict pain, to destroy his spirit. But Veit was not guilty of weakness — he was innocent and strong.

The battle raged on. Veit used the landscape as his defense — ducking behind walls, climbing over debris, and using every trick he had learned on his journey. The Shadow lunged, and Veit dodged. The Shadow swung its sword, and Veit rolled aside. He would not shoot back, he would not blame or accuse — he would simply resist and endure.

"You are insane!" the Shadow screamed. "Why do you fight? What cause drives you?"

"The cause of good," Veit said. "You may expose my fear, but you will never erase my hope."

The Shadow fought with evil intent, a creature of pure chaos and horror. It tried every scheme — to betray Veit's trust, to trigger his doubt, to fill him with shock and guilt. It hurled false accusation and nasty insult. It tried to exclude Veit, to exile him, to make him suffer in misery and denial.

But Veit held firm. He was caught in the storm, battered and bruised, but not broken. The crime the Shadow committed — the abuse of power, the neglect of justice, the ugly warfare it waged — only made Veit more determined.

Then, in a moment of quiet, Veit held up the three crystal pieces. They began to glow — brighter and brighter — until the light was blinding. The Shadow let out a scream of fury and retreat. The light pushed it back, step by step, until it stumbled and fell.

"No!" the Shadow cried. "This is wrong! This is unfair!"

"What is wrong," Veit said calmly, "is what you have done. You destroy and damage and inflict pain. You ignore the suffering of others. You oppose everything good. You have earned no mercy."

The crystal's light consumed the Shadow. It dissolved like smoke in the wind, leaving nothing behind but a dark stain on the ground. The tornado weakened. The storm began to fade.

A sheriff and a small army of soldier arrived moments later, led by a brave warrior fox. They had been tracking the Shadow for months. A march through the hills had brought them here just in time.

"Are you hurt?" asked the sheriff.

"I am fine," Veit said. "The Shadow is gone."

The sheriff nodded. "You will need to stand as a witness at a trial. This creature has a long record of crime — assault, accident, damage, and worse. It was an inmate once, escaped from a high-security prison. There is a lawsuit pending and a penalty to be paid. The judge will want your testimony."

"I will tell everything," Veit said. "I will not make an excuse or offer a false account. I will not deny what happened. The case is clear."

The soldiers arrest the last of the Shadow's followers — a mad band of thieves who had acted as spy and saboteur. They were angry and vicious, and one tried to shove a guard and argue his way free. Another was rude and would swear at the officers. A veteran among them — a scarred wolf with negative eyes — tried to start a riot, but was quickly restrained. They were all taken in chains, their weapons — whip, sword, pistol, rifle, and even a hidden bomb — confiscated. The police secured the area, and a bunker was uncovered nearby, filled with stolen goods. Each suspect faced a charge of illegal activity. The judge would reject any excuse and prevent them from causing more trouble. The Shadow's siege of terror had left a trail of damage — families torn apart by divorce and grief, lives spoil by greed. But now it was over. One could not undo the past, but one could enlist in the fight for a better future. And any who called the Shadow a hero were nothing but a liar — it was the fault of the darkness, not the light. Justice had been served.

Veit sat on a rock and caught his breath. His fur was singed, his paws were sore, and his heart still pounded.

The battle had been fatal for the Shadow, but Veit had survived. He had not used violence — he had used light.

He had refuse to become what the Shadow was. He had disagree with hatred, rebel against cruelty, and chosen mercy over revenge. He had been forced to remove the Shadow not through warfare, but through the power of the crystal and the courage of his heart.

The tragic chapter was over. But its lesson would remain: evil cannot be fought with evil. Only light can drive out darkness.

Veit picked up his bag. The crystal pieces hummed softly inside. He wiped the dust from his face and looked toward the horizon.

Home was close. And nothing would stop him now.

He would not topple under the weight of what had happened. He would march on, one step at a time, and rescue the peace that the world deserved.

The storm had passed. The sky was clearing. And Veit walked on, into the light.

Chapter 19:
The Return Home

The forest appeared on the horizon like an old friend waving from a distance. Veit's heart leaped. After months of travel, after every challenge and every miracle along the way, he was finally coming home.

He walked through the familiar gate and down the old path. The trees were taller than he remembered, and the world around him seemed both the same and somehow changed. Or perhaps it was Veit who had changed. He was no longer the same young fox who had left — he had grown, evolve in ways he could not yet fully admit.

His family was waiting.

His mother saw him first. She let out a cry of joy and ran to embrace him. His father followed, wrapping his arms around them both. His brother and sister joined in, and soon the entire family was together again, laughing and crying at once. It was a reunion like no other — a moment of pure, genuine happiness.

"You came back," his mother whispered. "You really came back."

"I promised I would," Veit said with a smile. "And I keep my promises."

He placed the three crystal pieces on the ground. They fit together perfectly, as if they had never been apart. The crystal was intact — whole, perfect, and glowing with a warm golden light. It was the final moment of the quest, and it was beautiful.

"Now," Veit said, "I must combine them."

He closed his eyes and held the crystal tight. A pulse of energy rippled outward — through the trees, through the earth, through the air. The forest came alive. Flowers bloomed. Birds sang. The creek sparkled. The ancient balance had been restored.

The Elder Owl watched from a high branch and nodded slowly. "You have done what no one else could," he said. "You found the pieces, carried them across the world, and brought them home. That is a success worth celebrating."

Veit opened his eyes. He looked at the faces around him — his family, his friends, the creatures of the forest — and felt a wave of gratitude so deep it took his breath away.

"I could not have done it alone," Veit said. "Every someone I met along the way helped me. Every gift of kindness, every gesture of grace, every act of help made this possible. I want to thank every one of them."

He began to recall the journey — every person and creature who had made a difference. The old duck who let him borrow a canoe. The captain who carried him across the sea. The farmer who taught him patience. The professor who taught him to think. The queen who chose to trust. Each had played a crucial part.

"We must never forget what happened," Veit said. "We must remind ourselves that the world is worth protecting. We must devote ourselves to make it better — to enhance what is good, enrich what is beautiful, and repair what is broken."

The Elder Owl spread his wings. "The crystal is more than a thing of power," he said. "It is a link between the past and the future. It will sustain this forest and protect its creatures for generations. But it will only thrive if you — all of you — choose to care for it."

Veit nodded. "I pledge to do my part. I will inspire others, empower them to act, and enable change wherever I can. I will foster trust, embrace truth, and stand for what is right. I will not be perfect — I will make mistake after mistake — but I will learn from each one and become better."

"That," said the Owl, "is the only viable path. And let me confirm something: the crystal will only work for those with the right attitude — those who are humble and proud at the same time, proud of what they have done but humble enough to admit they still have much to learn. Let me also urge you to include every creature in this effort. We all depend on one another."

Veit's response was simple: "I will."

The days that followed were full of joy and comfort. Veit helped rebuild the parts of the forest that had been damaged by the Shadow's darkness. He would fix a broken bridge, replace a fallen fence, and gather stones to mend a wall. He learned to settle dilemma with patience, to share what he had, and to receive help with humble grace. It did not occur to him to feel sorry for himself — instead, he felt bless by every new day. He worked to convince others that the forest was their priority too, and the real reward was seeing them believe it.

He made a pact with the creatures of the forest: to protect the crystal, to provide for each other, and to ensure that no one was ever left behind. It was a mutual agreement, a bond of loyalty and purpose.

"I give you my word," Veit said. "I will assist anyone in need, donate my time and effort, and involve every creature in the decisions that affect us all. We are equal, and every voice matters."

The forest prosper. New paths were built, new gardens planted, new friendships formed. The crystal's light spread through the land, touching every corner. A sense of purity and peace settled over everything. The world felt whole again.

One evening, Veit sat beneath his old oak tree and looked up at the stars. He thought about the choice he had made — to leave home, to face danger, and to bring the crystal back. It had been the hardest thing he had ever done, but also the most rewarding.

He pulled out his diary and began to write. He wanted to save every memory, every moment, every lesson. He wanted to present his story to the world — not for fame or glory, but so that others might gain the courage to start their own quest.

"The truth is simple," he wrote. "The world will test you. It will ask you to decide who you are and what you stand for. It will unveil your fears and unfold your strengths. You will stumble. You will doubt. But if you rely on the people who love you, if you keep your purpose close and your heart open, you will find your way."

He paused and added: "I am not a hero. I am just a fox who made a choice. And that choice — to be brave, to be kind, to be true — is one that any creature can make."

His mother brought him a cup of warm tea. "Are you okay?" she asked.

"I am more than okay," Veit said. "I am glad. I am grateful. And I am home."

She sat beside him. "You know," she said, "the greatest miracle is not the crystal. It is you — who you have become."

Veit smiled. He felt the comfort of her presence, the relief of being safe, and the quiet joy of a life well lived. The quest was over, but its benefit would last a lifetime.

He closed his diary and looked out at the forest. The crystal glowed softly in the distance, a beacon of hope and light.

"I myself am changed," he whispered. "And I will change the world, one small act at a time."

The stars shone above. The forest was at peace. And Veit the Fox — humble, loyal, and truly brave — rested at last.

But this is not the end. It is only the beginning. For every year brings new challenges, every option a new path, and every moment a new chance to make the world a better place.

The crystal's light will never fade — as long as there is someone willing to carry it.

And so, the moral of the story is this: you are capable of more than you know. You can alter your life, improve your world, and develop into the person you were always meant to become. All it takes is a single choice — to emerge from the shadows, to expand your heart, and to embody the courage that lives inside every one of us.

Do not forget. Do not lose hope. And never, ever stop walking.

The future is waiting.

It always was.

This is Veit's gift to you: the release of fear, the embrace of truth, and the quiet praise of a life lived with purpose and grace.

May you thrive. May you prosper. May you find your own crystal — and carry its light into the world.

With love, and with gratitude,

Veit.

— The End —

"I suggest you do what I did: take the first step, and trust that the path will unfold beneath your feet. That is the only surprise worth waiting for — the one you create."

Veit the Fox, from the dedication of his memoir, written many year later, in the inner room of his old oak tree, surrounded by those he love most. He had long since retire from adventuring, but his spirit lived on in every youth who heard his tale and chose to follow the light.

He never did renew the quest. He never had to. The crystal was safe, the forest was whole, and the world was at peace. And that was enough.

He gave a small wave, closed the door, and reopen his diary to write one last line:

"Witness this: a life of merit, purity, and joy. I would not replace a single moment. I would not change a single thing. Every mistake was a lesson. Every apology was a bridge. Either way, it was all worth it."

And with a final smile, Veit set down his pen and went to sleep — safe, glad, and at peace, in the home he had fought so hard to protect.

"Okay," he murmured. "That is truly the end."

And it was.